THE UNIVERSITY OF ALABAMA®
COOKBOOK

BROWNE MERCER

PHOTOGRAPHS BY ZAC WILLIAMS

GIBBS SMITH
TO ENRICH AND INSPIRE HUMANKIND

First Edition
15 14 13 12 11   5 4 3 2

Text © 2011 Browne Mercer
Photographs © 2011 Zac Williams

Published by
Gibbs Smith
P.O. Box 667
Layton, Utah 84041

1.800.835.4993 orders
www.gibbs-smith.com

Designed by Rita Sowins/Sowins Design
Printed and bound in China

Gibbs Smith books are printed on either recycled, 100% post-consumer waste, FSC-certified papers or on paper produced from sustainable PEFC-certified forest/controlled wood source. Learn more at www.pefc.org.

Library of Congress Cataloging-in-Publication Data

Mercer, Browne.
   The University of Alabama cookbook / Browne Mercer ; photographs by Zac Williams. — 1st ed.
       p. cm.
   ISBN 978-1-4236-2145-4
1. Cooking, American—Southern Style. 2. Cooking—Alabama—Tuscaloosa. 3. University of Alabama. 4. Cookbooks. I. Title.
   TX715.2.S68M469 2011
   641.59761'84—dc22
                          2011003605

For the front cover recipe, contact the publisher at info@gibbs-smith.com

CONTENTS

DIPS

Rollin' with the Tide® Salsa 4

Vidalia Onion Dip 7

Mustard Dip 8

Bammy-Bound Dip 11

White Bean Dip 12

APPETIZERS

Give 'em Hell, Alabama®
Deviled Eggs 15

Grit-Stuffed Mushrooms 16

Crimson Cheese Crisps 19

Red Elephant Snacks 20

Old South Sausage Swirls 23

MAIN COURSES

B.B.R. Pork 24

War Chicken Wings 27

Bama® Bourbon-Glazed
Pork Tenderloin 28

The Bama® Lotta 31

Drown 'em Tide Brisket 32

Got Thirteen? Chili 34

SALADS AND VEGGIES

Olive Salad 37

Red-and-White Bean Salad 38

The Capstone Coleslaw 41

Dixie's Football Pride Potato Salad 42

Rammer Jammer Baked Beans 45

Crimson Flame Black-Eyed Peas 46

SWEETS AND BEVERAGES

Roll Tide® Roll Doughnut Holes 49

Million-Dollar Chocolate
Pound Cake 50

Big Al's Peanut Butter Bars 53

Roll on to Victory Lemon
Pound Cake 54

Heavenly Hash Cake 57

Yellow Hammer 58

Bama® Bomb 61

Cranberry Punch 62

Rollin' with the Tide®
SALSA

Ingredients

12 Roma tomatoes, diced

²/₃ cup chopped shallots

2 cloves garlic, minced

2 jalapeños, seeded and finely chopped

¹/₂ cup fresh cilantro, chopped

¹/₂ cup fresh parsley, chopped

¹/₂ cup extra virgin olive oil

¹/₂ teaspoon granulated garlic

1 teaspoon salt

1 teaspoon pepper

Tortilla chips

Combine all ingredients except tortilla chips in a large bowl and refrigerate until ready to serve. Serve with chips.

❖ Serves 6–8 ❖

Vidalia Onion
DIP

Ingredients

2 cups chopped Vidalia onions

3 cups grated Swiss cheese

2 cups Hellman's mayonnaise

2 tablespoons minced garlic

Salt and pepper, to taste

Crackers, of choice

❖ Serves 6–8 ❖

Preheat oven to 325 degrees. In a large bowl, mix all ingredients together. Place in a shallow 8 x 8-inch baking dish and bake for 20 minutes. At the end of the baking time, if you want a little color, turn oven to broil for about 5 minutes. Serve with crackers.

Variation: If you would like to offer dip as individual servings, bake as directed and then scoop into 6–8 ramekins or small decorative bowls and serve.

Mustard
DIP

Ingredients

2 cups sour cream

¾ cup Creole mustard

¼ cup minced shallot

2 tablespoons chopped green onion

1 teaspoon Creole seasoning

❖ Serves 6–8 ❖

Combine sour cream, mustard, shallot, onion, and Creole seasoning in medium bowl. Refrigerate for at least 1 hour before serving. This dip is great with grilled smoked sausage.

Bammy-Bound
DIP

Ingredients

5 slices bacon

4 medium Vidalia onions, chopped

1 tablespoon butter

2 cups sour cream

1 teaspoon Worcestershire sauce

1 teaspoon balsamic vinegar

$1^1/_2$ teaspoons granulated garlic

Salt and pepper, to taste

Chips, of choice

In a large frying pan, cook bacon until crisp. Chop and set aside. In same pan, cook onions in butter and bacon grease until caramelized—they will be dark brown, almost black. Allow to cool. Transfer onions to a large bowl and combine with remaining ingredients to make a dip. Refrigerate for at least 2 hours or overnight before serving. Serve with chips.

❖ Serves 6–8 ❖

White Bean
DIP

Ingredients

1 can (16 ounces) white
   cannellini beans,
   rinsed and drained

$1^{1}/_{2}$ tablespoons lemon juice

$1^{1}/_{2}$ tablespoons extra
   virgin olive oil

1 large clove garlic

$^{3}/_{4}$ teaspoon cumin

1 tablespoon chopped
   fresh dill

1 teaspoon minced
   lemon zest

Salt and pepper, to taste

Pita chips or crackers

Purée first 5 ingredients in a food processor or blender until smooth. Transfer to a medium bowl and stir in dill and zest. Season with salt and pepper. Serve with pita chips or crackers.

❖ Serves 6–8 ❖

Give 'em Hell, Alabama®
DEVILED EGGS

Ingredients

1 dozen hard-boiled eggs

1 tablespoon chopped shallot

1/4 cup Hellman's mayonnaise

2 teaspoons Dijon mustard

2 tablespoons Sriracha hot sauce

1 teaspoon lime juice

1/4 teaspoon granulated garlic

Salt and pepper, to taste

Paprika

❖ Makes 24 eggs ❖

Shell eggs, cut in half, and gently remove yolks. In a large bowl, chop yolks and mix in the remaining ingredients except paprika. Spoon mixture back into egg whites and place on a platter. Sprinkle with paprika and refrigerate until ready to serve.

Grit-Stuffed
MUSHROOMS

Ingredients

- 1 1/2 pounds fresh medium-size button mushrooms
- 3 tablespoons butter
- 3 tablespoons extra virgin olive oil
- 6 tablespoons finely chopped green onion
- 9 cloves garlic, minced
- 3 teaspoons chopped fresh parsley
- 3 teaspoons salt
- 1 1/2 teaspoons cracked pepper
- 3 cups cooked grits

❖ Serves 6–8 ❖

Preheat oven to 350 degrees. Remove mushroom stems; chop them into small pieces and sauté in butter and oil in a large frying pan with onion. Add garlic, parsley, salt, and pepper and sauté for 2 more minutes. Stir in grits until thoroughly combined. This mixture should be thick.

Stuff mushroom caps with grit mixture and place on a baking sheet pan lined with parchment paper. Bake for 15–20 minutes.

Crimson
CHEESE CRISPS

Ingredients

2 sticks Imperial margarine

**2 cups grated extra sharp
cheddar cheese**

2 cups flour

$^1/_2$ teaspoon cayenne pepper

$^1/_2$ teaspoon salt

2 cups Rice Krispies

1 cup pecan pieces

❖ Serves 6–8 ❖

Preheat oven to 350 degrees. Using a mixer, cream margarine and cheese until fluffy. Add flour, cayenne, and salt. Then add Rice Krispies and pecans. Roll into 1-inch balls and place on a baking sheet lined with parchment paper. Lightly press balls with a fork and bake for 13–15 minutes, or until lightly browned. Loosen from the sheet while still warm.

Red Elephant
SNACKS

Ingredients

1 stick butter

1 teaspoon garlic salt

½ teaspoon onion salt

2 tablespoons
   Worcestershire sauce

2 cups Wheat Chex

2 cups Rice Chex

2 cups Corn Chex

2 cups Cheerios

1 pound mixed nuts

1 cup pretzel sticks

1 cup Melba toasts

1 cup sesame sticks

❖ Serves 6–8 ❖

Preheat oven to 200 degrees. Melt butter in a medium saucepan and add seasonings. Combine remaining ingredients in a large roasting pan and pour butter over mixture. Stir well and bake for at least 2 hours, stirring every 20 minutes. Allow to cool before serving.

Old South
SAUSAGE SWIRLS

Ingredients

4 cups flour

¼ cup cornmeal

¼ cup sugar

2 tablespoons baking powder

2 teaspoons salt

⅔ cup vegetable oil

⅔ to 1 cup milk

2 pounds ground hot sausage

❖ Serves 6–8 ❖

In a large bowl, sift dry ingredients together. Blend in oil. Add enough milk to make stiff dough. Roll out dough into two thin 10 x 18-inch rectangles. Spread sausage on dough and roll up, starting with the 10-inch side. Wrap rolls in plastic wrap and chill well.

Preheat oven to 350 degrees. Slice rolls into ¼-inch pieces and place on baking sheet lined with parchment paper. Bake for 15–20 minutes, or until lightly browned.

B.B.R.
PORK

Bama® Butt Rub (B.B.R.)

2 tablespoons salt

2 tablespoons pepper

4 tablespoons
   granulated onion

6 tablespoons
   granulated garlic

2 tablespoons chili powder

2 tablespoons paprika

Ingredients

B.B.R.

6 pound Boston butt

❖ Serves 6–8 ❖

Combine all rub ingredients and set aside.

Preheat grill to 250 degrees. Rub the B.B.R. on all sides of the meat. Place meat on grill, fat side up, and cook for approximately $1^{1}/_{2}$ hours per pound. Cooking times vary from grill to grill, so as the cooking time ends, watch the meat carefully. Cover with foil if the meat becomes too dark before desired internal temperature. The internal temperature should be 180 degrees if you want to serve sliced pork and 205 degrees for pulled pork.

War Chicken
WINGS

Ingredients

6 pounds chicken wings

$1/2$ cup olive oil

2 cups pineapple juice

1 cup orange juice

1 teaspoon granulated garlic

$1/2$ teaspoon pepper

$1/2$ teaspoon salt

2 cups Crystal Hot Sauce

2 teaspoons butter

❖ Serves 6–8 ❖

Preheat oven to 400 degrees. Wash and separate wings. Put chicken in a 12 x 20-inch aluminum foil pan and add next 6 ingredients. Cover pan and cook for 45 minutes. Remove wings from oven and drain, reserving 1 cup cooking liquid.

In a small bowl, combine hot sauce, butter, and reserved liquid to make a basting sauce. Place wings on a foil-lined baking sheet and turn the oven to low broil. Broil, uncovered, for approximately 30 minutes; turning and basting every few minutes until crispy.

Bama® Bourbon-Glazed
PORK TENDERLOIN

Ingredients

1 cup pineapple juice

3 ounces bourbon

1/2 cup light brown sugar

Salt and pepper, to taste

2 pork tenderloins

Olive oil

Granulated garlic, to taste

❖ Serves 6–8 ❖

Place pineapple juice, bourbon, and sugar in a small saucepan and cook over medium heat. Stir and reduce by half. Season with salt and pepper.

Trim pork loin. Drizzle pork with oil and add granulated garlic, salt, and pepper. Preheat grill to 400 degrees (medium high) and sear pork for 5 minutes on each side. Reduce heat and baste meat with glaze, turning every 3 minutes or so, until pork is done, about 20–25 minutes on low heat. Slice into 1/4-inch slices and place on a platter.

The Bama®
LOTTA

Ingredients

1 fresh focaccia round

Olive Salad (see page 37)

2 ounces provolone

2 ounces salami

2 ounces pepperoni

1 ounce prosciutto

2 ounces fresh mozzarella

❖ Serves 2 ❖

Slice bread in half so that you have a top and a bottom. Spread a layer of Olive Salad on the bottom half of the bread. Place provolone slices, salami, pepperoni, and prosciutto on the salad then top with fresh mozzarella. Spread a layer of salad on the top half of the bread and place on the sandwich. Wrap tightly in plastic wrap and place in refrigerator for at least 2 hours. Slice in wedges and serve.

Drown 'em Tide
BRISKET

Ingredients

1 can (12 ounces)
  beef consommé

1 cup water

3/4 cup Worcestershire sauce

1/3 cup apple cider vinegar

1/3 cup vegetable oil

2 teaspoons granulated garlic

1 1/2 teaspoons chili powder

1/2 teaspoon Tabasco

4 bay leaves

5 to 6 pound brisket

Bama® Butt Rub (see page 24)

Au Jus

2 1/2 cups beef stock

1 carrot

2 stalks celery

1/2 yellow onion

❖ Serves 6–8 ❖

Combine consommé and water in a medium saucepan and bring to boil. Remove from heat and stir in next 7 ingredients, cover, and let the sauce stand at room temperature for at least 4 hours.

Preheat oven to 300 degrees. Trim off excess fat from brisket and completely cover meat with rub. Place brisket in shallow baking pan, fat side up, and bake uncovered for 1 hour. Reduce heat to 250 degrees; pour sauce over meat and cover. Cook 4–5 hours, basting every hour. It takes approximately an hour per pound of brisket to cook. Remove brisket from pan and let cool, reserving 1/2 cup drippings. This recipe can be made a day ahead. Just reheat the meat on the grill at your tailgate party.

To make the au jus; combine the reserved drippings with beef stock and vegetables in a large saucepan. Bring to a boil and cook until vegetables are soft, 15–20 minutes. Strain liquid. When you are ready to serve, thinly slice meat on the bias and pour warm au jus over sliced meat. Serve with horseradish sauce.

Variation: This recipe makes a great French dip sandwich.

Horseradish Sauce

1 cup sour cream

**$^1/_2$ cup freshly ground
  horseradish**

$^1/_4$ cup Creole mustard

Salt and pepper, to taste

Combine ingredients together in a small bowl. Refrigerate until ready to use.

❖ **Makes approximately
1$^1/_2$ cups** ❖

33

Got Thirteen?
CHILI

Ingredients

1 pound lean ground beef

Salt and pepper, to taste

1 large onion, chopped

13 cloves garlic, chopped

**1 jalapeño, seeded
  and chopped**

**$1/2$ cup chopped
  green onions**

**1 can (16 ounces)
  tomato sauce**

**1 can (16 ounces) dark
  red kidney beans,
  rinsed and drained**

**1 can (16 ounces)
  white kidney beans,
  rinsed and drained**

2 cups water

3 tablespoons flour

Brown beef in large stock pot, seasoning with salt and pepper. Add onion and cook until translucent. Add garlic and jalapeño to pot and cook 2–3 minutes. Next, add green onions, tomato sauce, beans, water, and flour. Stir and bring to a simmer. Lower heat, cover, and cook for 1 hour.

Variation: Substitute ground venison for the ground beef.

 Serves 6–8

Olive
SALAD

Ingredients

1½ cups chopped
  green olives

1 cup chopped niçoise olives

¼ cup chopped capers

¼ cup chopped
  pepperoncini peppers

¼ cup chopped green
  onions, white part only

1 stalk celery, chopped

1 carrot, chopped

2 cloves garlic, minced

1 teaspoon oregano

1 teaspoon pepper

½ teaspoon celery seed

¾ cup extra virgin olive oil

¼ cup canola oil

Combine all ingredients together in a large bowl and refrigerate overnight.

❖ Makes approximately
4 cups, or enough for 4
Bama® Lotta sandwiches ❖

Red-and-White
BEAN SALAD

Ingredients

¾ cup sugar

⅓ cup olive oil

⅔ cup apple cider vinegar

½ teaspoon pepper

1 teaspoon salt

¼ teaspoon oregano

¼ teaspoon celery seed

1 can (16 ounces) white kidney beans, rinsed and drained

1 can (16 ounces) dark red kidney beans, rinsed and drained

1 can (16 ounces) garbanzo beans, rinsed and drained

1 small white onion, chopped

1 green bell pepper, chopped

2 celery stalks, chopped

Combine first 7 ingredients into a large bowl and stir. Add beans, onion, bell pepper, and celery to bowl; stir to combine. Refrigerate overnight before serving.

❖ Serves 6–8 ❖

The Capstone
COLESLAW

Ingredients

2 bags (16 ounces each) coleslaw

1/2 cup chopped shallot

1/4 cup jalapeño, seeded and chopped

1 red bell pepper, seeded and chopped

Dressing

1/2 cup sour cream

1/2 cup Creole mustard

2 tablespoons lemon juice

4 teaspoons sugar

2 teaspoons salt

1 teaspoon pepper

❖ Serves 6–8 ❖

Combine coleslaw, shallot, jalapeño, and bell pepper together in a large bowl. Combine dressing ingredients in a small bowl and pour over slaw. Stir well and chill before serving.

Dixie's Football Pride
POTATO SALAD

Ingredients

**5 pounds Yukon
gold potatoes**

**1 bunch green onions,
chopped**

1 small white onion, chopped

3 stalks of celery, diced

1 teaspoon yellow mustard

**3 teaspoons apple
cider vinegar**

**2 tablespoons extra virgin
olive oil**

$^1/_2$ cup Hellman's mayonnaise

**4 slices bacon, cooked
and crumbled**

**3 tablespoons
chopped parsley**

Salt and pepper, to taste

In a large stock pot, boil potatoes until fork tender, drain, cool, and peel. Dice potatoes and combine with onions and celery in a large bowl and set aside.

In a small bowl, combine mustard, vinegar, oil, and mayonnaise. Toss together with vegetables and add bacon, parsley, salt, and pepper.

❖ Serves 6–8 ❖

Rammer Jammer
BAKED BEANS

Ingredients

1 pound ground beef

1 white onion, diced

2 tablespoons minced garlic

2 cans (28 ounces each) Bush's Maple-Cured Baked Beans

$2/3$ cup crushed tomatoes

2 tablespoons yellow mustard

1 tablespoon Worcestershire sauce

$1/8$ teaspoon granulated garlic

$1/4$ teaspoon pepper

Salt, to taste

❖ Serves 6–8 ❖

Preheat oven to 350 degrees. In a large frying pan, brown beef and onion; add garlic and beans. Stir in remaining ingredients and place in an 8 x 12-inch oven-proof casserole dish. Bake for 45 minutes or until hot and bubbly.

Crimson Flame
BLACK-EYED PEAS

Ingredients

1 pound dried black-
 eyed peas

1 medium yellow
 onion, chopped

1/2 green bell pepper,
 chopped

4 stalks celery, chopped

6 cloves garlic, chopped

2 tablespoons olive oil

1 pound ham steak,
 cooked and diced

2 teaspoons dried thyme

1 can (8 ounces)
 tomato sauce

2 quarts water

1/2 teaspoon cayenne pepper

1 teaspoon pepper

2 teaspoons salt

Soak black-eyed peas overnight and rinse. Sauté onion, bell pepper, celery, and garlic in a large stockpot. Add ham, thyme, and tomato sauce. Heat thoroughly. Stir in black-eyed peas and then add water and seasonings. Bring to a boil, lower heat to a simmer, and cover. Cook for 2 hours, or until tender, stirring frequently. Add additional water as needed.

❖ Serves 6–8 ❖

Roll Tide® Roll
DOUGHNUT HOLES

Ingredients

2 cups flour

1 tablespoon baking powder

1/2 teaspoon salt

1 teaspoon nutmeg

1 teaspoon cinnamon

1 egg

1/2 cup sugar

2 tablespoons orange zest

4 tablespoons shortening

1/3 cup evaporated milk

1/4 cup water

1/4 cup powdered sugar, sifted

1/2 teaspoon cinnamon

❖ Serves 6–8 ❖

Preheat oven to 400 degrees. Sift first 5 ingredients together in a medium bowl. Beat together egg, sugar, and zest in the bowl of a stand mixer. Add in flour mixture, shortening, milk, and water and combine. Beat for 2 minutes. Using a 3/4-ounce or small cookie scoop, drop balls of dough into the cups of a greased mini muffin pan to make doughnut hole-size balls. Bake 15–20 minutes.

Combine powdered sugar and cinnamon in a large bowl. Toss doughnut holes in the mixture as soon as they come out of the oven.

Million-Dollar
CHOCOLATE POUND CAKE

Ingredients

1 cup butter

$^1/_2$ cup shortening

3 cups sugar

5 eggs

3 cups flour

$^1/_2$ teaspoon baking powder

$^1/_2$ teaspoon salt

4 heaping tablespoons
cocoa powder

1 cup milk

1 tablespoon vanilla

Icing

$^2/_3$ cup butter, softened

1 teaspoon vanilla

$^2/_3$ cup powdered sugar

1 tablespoon milk

1 heaping tablespoon
cocoa powder

Preheat oven to 325 degrees. Using a mixer, cream butter, shortening, and sugar. Add eggs. Combine flour, baking powder, salt, and cocoa in a medium bowl. Add dry ingredients to the butter mixture, alternating with the milk. Add vanilla. Pour batter into a well-greased and floured Bundt pan. Bake 1 hour and 20 minutes.

Combine icing ingredients together in a large bowl and then drizzle over cake while still warm.

Variation: Use mini Bundt pans for individual servings. Change baking time to 40–45 minutes.

❖ Serves 10–12 ❖

Big Al's
PEANUT BUTTER BARS

Ingredients

2 cups flour

1/2 cup brown sugar

1/4 teaspoon salt

**1/4 cup butter, room
temperature**

1 cup peanut butter

1 egg

1 cup milk chocolate pieces

1 teaspoon butter

**1 can (14 ounces) sweetened
condensed milk**

Preheat oven to 350 degrees. Combine flour, brown sugar, and salt in a large bowl. Add 1/4 cup butter, peanut butter, and then egg to make a thick batter. Press 2/3 of mixture into bottom of greased 9 x 13-inch baking pan.

Melt chocolate with 1 teaspoon butter and milk in a small saucepan. Pour over peanut butter mixture in the baking pan. Sprinkle the remaining peanut butter mixture over chocolate mixture. Bake for 20 minutes or until golden brown. Let cool before cutting into bars.

❖ Makes 24 bars ❖

Roll on to Victory
LEMON POUND CAKE

Ingredients

1 cup butter, softened

1/4 cup sugar

3 eggs

2 teaspoons baking powder

1 teaspoon almond extract

2 tablespoons lemon zest

1 cup milk

3 cups flour

Glaze

3 cups powdered sugar

3/4 cup lemon juice

❖ Serves 10–12 ❖

Preheat oven to 325 degrees. Using a mixer, cream butter and sugar until light and fluffy. Add eggs, one at a time. Add baking powder, almond extract, and lemon zest. Add milk and flour, alternating 1/3 at a time, and mix well. Pour batter into a greased and floured Bundt pan. Bake for 1 hour.

While the cake is baking, mix together powdered sugar and lemon juice. Set aside. When cake is done, remove from oven. Poke holes in top of cake using a wooden skewer and pour 3/4 of glaze on top of cake. Cool cake completely in the pan. Invert cake onto a serving platter and pour remaining glaze over the cake.

Variation: Use mini Bundt pans for individual servings. Change baking time to 40 minutes.

Heavenly Hash
CAKE

Ingredients

4 eggs, slightly beaten

2 cups sugar

2 sticks butter, melted

4 tablespoons cocoa powder

$1/2$ cup self-rising flour

2 cups pecan pieces

2 teaspoons vanilla

Mini marshmallows

Topping

**1 box (16 ounces)
    powdered sugar**

4 tablespoons butter, melted

4 tablespoons cocoa powder

$1/2$ cup heavy cream

❖ Serves 12 ❖

Preheat oven 350 degrees. Using a large bowl, beat eggs and sugar together; add butter. Mix in cocoa powder and flour. Fold in pecans and add vanilla. Bake in a greased 9 x 13-inch pan for 40 minutes. Sprinkle marshmallows on top of hot cake when it comes out of the oven.

To make the topping; combine powdered sugar, butter, cocoa, and cream in a large bowl; pour over marshmallows. Let cool before cutting into bars.

Yellow
HAMMER

Ingredients

36 ounces pineapple juice

18 ounces orange juice

12 ounces white grape juice

6 ounces apple cider

1 tablespoon vanilla extract

Juice from one lime

❖ Serves 6 ❖

Combine all ingredients in large pitcher and pour over ice in glasses.

Note: This nonalcoholic version of a yellow hammer is a perfect alternative for those who prefer alcohol-free drinks.

Bama®
BOMB

Ingredients

1 jar (10 ounces) of maraschino cherries

1 teaspoon almond extract

Apple cider

❖ Serves 6–8 ❖

Pour half of the cherry juice out of the jar. Add almond extract, then fill jar with apple cider. Refrigerate for 2 to 3 days before serving.

Note: These almond-flavored cherries are a tasty nonalcoholic substitute for the alcohol-infused Bama® Bomb.

Cranberry
PUNCH

Ingredients

**1 pint cranberry
juice cocktail**

6 ounces pineapple juice

6 tablespoons lemon juice

³/₄ cup sugar

28 ounces ginger ale, chilled

❖ Serves 6-8 ❖

Combine cranberry juice, pineapple juice, and lemon juice in a large pitcher. Stir in sugar until dissolved. Add ginger ale and stir.

BROWNE MERCER attended the University of Alabama. He is a self-taught chef and an established cake decorator. Browne's true love of food comes from his grandmother and shows every day in the many unique dishes he prepares. He honed his culinary skills with the help of his wife, Chef Missy, and they jointly own two restaurants and a bakery in the Old Cloverdale district of Montgomery, Alabama.